Deep

Gossip

Johns Hopkins:

Poetry and Fiction

Wyatt Prunty,

General Editor

Sidney Wade

Deep Gossip

new and
selected poems

jh

Johns Hopkins

University Press

Baltimore

This book has been brought to publication with the generous assistance of the John T. Irwin Poetry and Fiction Endowed Fund.

Printed in the United States of America on acid-free paper
9 8 7 6 5 4 3 2 1

Johns Hopkins University Press
2715 North Charles Street
Baltimore, Maryland 21218-4363
www.press.jhu.edu

Library of Congress Cataloging-in-Publication Data

Names: Wade, Sidney, author.
Title: Deep gossip : new and selected poems / Sidney Wade.
Description: Baltimore : Johns Hopkins University Press, 2020. |
    Series: Johns Hopkins: poetry and fiction
Identifiers: LCCN 2019033924 | ISBN 9781421437873 (paperback ;
    acid-free paper) | ISBN 9781421437880 (ebook)
Classification: LCC PS3573.A337 A6 2020 | DDC 811/.54–dc23
LC record available at https://lccn.loc.gov/2019033924

A catalog record for this book is available from the British Library.

Special discounts are available for bulk purchases of this book. For more information, please contact Special Sales at specialsales@press.jhu.edu.

Johns Hopkins University Press uses environmentally friendly book materials, including recycled text paper that is composed of at least 30 percent post-consumer waste, whenever possible.

For my first and best teachers:

Willa Cather

Tinker Greene

David Huddle

With gratitude and love

Poetry is deep gossip. —Liam Rector

> ...All around us the water slips
> And gossips in its loose vernacular,
> Ferrying the smells of dead cod and tar.

—Sylvia Plath, "A Winter Ship"

Contents

from Straits & Narrows *(2013)*

from Bird Book *(2017)*

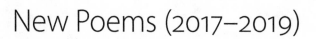

New Poems (2017–2019)

Fata Morgana

this morning

      winter sun pours

   through dark oaks

         on the avenue

     bright clean and rich

  and the soul soars

     and the body feels

every cell is about to break

             through illusion

   and disperse

      into pure shine

Three Voices

Chanterelle

My stubborn head breaks sod
and I spring up velvet gold,
my ceiling now the sky,
mycelium my mould.
My earthly frame is peach,
my odor apricot.
I appeal to heaven's eye
and ornament the plot.

Winter Wren

Tiny, plump, and brown,
I probe in soil and bark,
turning over matted leaves
and searching through the dark
for earthly stuff.
No one who came along
would guess I am the author
of a transcendental song.

Vole

I dream a brilliant dream
of roots and fruits and such.
I sister to the soil
and feather at her touch.
I wake and tunnel through
spring grass and thrips and gnats
and skylark in the fluid light
that screens the cryptic cat.

Bees

Little
engineers

foraging in
your morning amble,

you tumble
into the stars,

panicles,
and umbels

of our
blossoming

world,
emerging

in yellow
splendor,

caparisoned
in tiny

suns.
Fine fellows

of the humming
universe,

conversant
in generation,

dancing
your nation's

intelligence
forward

in rumor
and buzz,

forgive us
our trespass

against the sweet
green earth,

your habitat.
Our kind

can be blind
to just deserts.

Pollen

each spring
pollen stars
our cars

our roses
it pools
and sheens

the pavement
after rain
gold green

it cakes
the town
such power!

each grain
a small sun
sacred dust

tree semen
powdered lust
it stuffs

the nose
and makes
it run

"Human Food Consists Entirely of Souls"

Iglulik hunter Ivaluardjuk to Danish
ethnologist Knud Rasmussen, 1921

On my kitchen shelves
large mason jars are stuffed
with the white, gray, and buff
bodies of former selves

I pulled from the moss duff
in which they thrived—
porcini, boletus, lively
fruit that flourished in the rough

of the forest floor but who now lie
stiff and dried and tough,
entombed in glass so I
may savor the flavor of mortal slough.

Here, Kitty Kitty Kitty Kitty

sings the Bachman's sparrow
in an amusing mnemonic

for those who listen.
Others offer sonic

commentary on food:
Who cooks for you?

asks the barred owl
tending to her brood.

Drink your t-e-e-e-e-e
instructs the loud

and bossy towhee.
Potato chip! Potato chip!

squawk bright flocks
of goldfinch.

The hungry Carolina wren
likes to order three

Cheeseburger, Cheeseburger, Cheeseburger
in the spring,

when vocalistic
bird-bling

is sung
most linguistically,

when plentiful
rafts of seeds and insects

splinter up in shoals
to be winnowed

and swallowed.

Rosy Maple Moth

Bright yellow
and pink,

you look like
an exotic

piece of candy
hanging

on my screen
just below

the pistachio
green

luna moth.
You two

appear
distinctly

tasty,
so much so

I wonder
how either

survives
long enough

to breed
and pass on

your toothsome
genes.

Perhaps
you're tough,

or maybe
your flavor

is gruesome
in the extreme.

Such luck,
that fate

nudged
you together

on my porch,
ambassadors

from the great
penetralium

of mystery,
metaphors

of the beautiful
and sweet,

or the bitter
to eat.

Memento Mori

My home is beautified
by lovely husks—
the frames of snail and mollusc,
of corals that have died.

They grace sills, the upright
piano, the counter, ornamenting
my transient lot. Might
an alien god, in the event

of my demise, then pick
my house up, the hull of my self,
deem it beautiful, and stick
it on an outlandish shelf?

Birdwatching

Consider
the kestrel

lucent blue
on the wing

ochre-tinged
rufous

barred back
the black

and striking
white

borders
of the flaring

tail
the dark light

in the penetrating
eye

When I
watch

this miracle
in the air

or on a wire
all the snares

of the thorny world
disappear

Figure and Ground: Cryptic Camouflage and Visual Rhyme

The short and stocky
chicken-like rail
with a short, pointy,
triangular tail,

poking through reeds
and microflora,
foraging seeds
and small carnivora,

is the whinnying hen
with the marshy aura
of wetland and fen,
the fabulous sora.

32 Birds

- Ashy Minivet
- Bean Goose
- Besra
- Bimaculated Lark
- Black Baza
- Black-billed Capercaillie
- Black-necklaced Scimitar Babbler
- Brahminy Kite
- Brambling
- Bronzed Drongo
- Brown-breasted Bulbul
- Cabot's Tragopan
- Chinese Francolin
- Dusky Fulvetta
- Fairy Pitta
- Goosander
- Grey Treepie
- Kiritimati Shearwater
- Little Bustard
- Little Stint
- Masked Booby
- Mistle Thrush
- Plain Flowerpecker
- Red Avadavat
- Red-billed Leiothrix
- Relict Gull
- Speckled Piculet
- Tanimbar Corrella
- Vivid Niltava
- Wandering Tattler
- Whinchat
- Zitting Cisticola

Junco in Snow

Pink-beaked and gray, he sits atop
the railing as the flurries
swirl around him, then he hops
down to the ground and hurries

after crumbs the Canada jays
have chipped off the suet.
Low winter light slants in, the day
will be cold and fine. En route

to branches high and nether
he's fluffed up, cheeky, bold,
in fair or dreadful weather.
No creature in the wild dies old.

Nature Poets

We wander in sensible
shoes through foliage
and chiggers
and soberly contemplate
the figure

of a handsome oriole
whose flashy orange
and black suit astounds
the watching universe.
I wonder how

we can simply stand
and bless the outrageously beautiful
as we hold to the now
and ogle
this vision on the bough?

Seeing the Ophthalmologist

We are here to shed light
on our condition.

My pupils dilate.

We are here to brighten
the interior of the eye,
to map the macula.

We are here to enlighten
dark spots in the tissue,
dimples in the web.

We are here to measure
the growing cataract,
to assess approaching disaster.

More light! More light!

We are here to arrive at clarity,
to inspect interstitial ashes.

Year by year our charts thicken.

The heavy man beside me wheezes,
his bulk straining the wicker
of his chair.

We are here to probe the shadows
as we observe flashes
of light on the fringes of vision.

Here my chin rests in the frame
of the cutting-edge instrument
whose small breeze

is a spider kissing my wide-open eye.

Eye

The pair
fanned

out of the air
and landed

four feet
from our feet.

They chattered
to each other

in their woody
spoke-like

language
as we stood

still on the dike
and admired

their gray height,
their orange

eyes.
I stared

and compared
my eye

to theirs,
my tall pyre

of polite
vanities

to their bright
unhumanity,

my human
sight to their

split fields of vision,
fields of stubble,

all much smaller
than they used to be,

as all can see,
since we continually

strip, shear,
fleece, and skin,

leaving little
but rubble

for them
to forage in.

Then they
eased their forms

from the diminishing frame
and slipped away.

Skin

the living bag
we live in

unfurred
unfeathered

bare
to the air

crusted
and weathered

by time
by fear

first to parse
the grammar

of lust
or wasting

sack of blood
and fluid

when breached
will flood

or weep
as mother's

legs wept
she lay

naked
shaved

bed-bound
and drowning

in her body's
watery

conjugations
of the verb *to die*

she declined
in spirit

she swelled
in form

betrayed
by the welter

of assaults
on her frame

she called
on God

to come
and get her

great beached
weight

she prayed
her dear eyes

wrecked
confounded

by the grave
declensions

of earth-bound
flesh

Fabric

I just hung
my laundry
on the line
and now
it looks
like rain.

I read my book,
I watch
for drops
on the slowly
moving
pane.

*

Some say
time is airy
mass
through which
our bodies
pass.

The dry sand
trickles
still
through its
momentary
glass.

*

In the fine
drizzle
of a bleak
midwinter day,
a cardinal sizzles
on a branch,

carmine
fire,
oblique
to each moment's
mortal
avalanche.

Breath

Bed, playpen,
engine

of song—
long and lissome

or pestilent
and stout—

the poet
counts

your moments
and sings

the winsome
and arrogant

human body.
You are demigod,

zephyr,
whisper,

breeze;
inspiration,

strangled
wheeze.

You are
psyche,

spirit, soul,
in short,

the whole
retort,

the earthly
platform

of grace and sorrow.
Without you,

there's no
tomorrow.

Fear

The moon
lumbered slow

and heavy
in front

of the sun
Thunder

to our right
lightning

thrashing
the distant

black clouds
At last

in the eerie
green dark

our bare eyes
witnessed

the black
disk rimmed

with gold
with fine

red lines of fire
at the ragged

edge of the hole
that looked back

and we knew
the grand

weight of radiance
would return

like we knew
our own hands

yet when the gold
sliver finally

re-appeared
animal

relief gushed
out of lungs

compressed
by fear

we hadn't known
abided there

Blood Moon

A tree
molts red

leaves,
last meats

of the pale-eyed
year.

A cardinal
regards

the rim
and abides

on the shedding
limb.

Spring Blizzard in Denmark, Kansas

the savage prairie wind
shrieks and thrashes
the budding peach trees
around the old stone house
a furious creature
in elemental need
it slashes snow
slantways and batters
the already haggard
junipers and lilacs
which manage to stand
in the face of near disaster
as for years they have in the hands
of this backbreaking heartland

Nothing New

after W. H. Auden

There's nothing we can do about the lunatic, and so
We watch and wait and share our fears. The poor will always pay.
This too shall pass, we tell ourselves, but we don't really know.

Disaster makes good headlines, so he ratchets up the show.
The billionaires enrich themselves in all the games they play.
There's nothing we can do about the lunatic. And so

We buy new things and throw them out and buy some more, although
Our bodies can't seem to understand what Spirit has to say.
This too shall pass, we tell ourselves, but we don't really know.

Helpless children die in prisons and the filthy rich winds blow
Away the soil, the fields, the springs. Great Mother grieves. Decays.
There's nothing we can do about the lunatic, and so

Corruption feeds on ruined land, the garbage mountains grow.
The magnates cheer and assure themselves they're digging in to stay.
This too shall pass, we tell ourselves, but we don't really know.

Will justice, will rivers, disappear for good? Will violence go
for the vulnerable throat of the sacred, Living Way?
There's nothing we can do about the lunatic, and so
This too shall pass, we tell ourselves. But we don't really know.

Yellow-crowned Tyrannulet, Cock of the Rock, Northern Screamer

Sharp beaks, the shining eyes, the radiant songs,
numinous parables of light and feathers,
I swear, I could watch birds all day long.
The doctor recommended I immerse
my soul in songful stuff, but much of the time
I contemplate a different sublime:

The clueless greedy fuckwad at the helm
keeps on braying out his shitty piehole.
The witless fucking cocksplat overwhelms
and filthifies the air—he can't control
his douchebag self-regard. The lardass sits
on his golden crapper and tweets, *the stupid schmuck,*
the rambling asshole fuckmuppet cockwomble shit
he smears on every goddamned day. He's clusterfucked
the nation, flaying all his micro-thoughts
on asslick toadies, filthy dickless thugs,
the shitbag wankers stealing all we've got—
cheesedicks, shitstains, fucksticks, dickbags, ugh.

three small movements

tiny foghorn—
frog
in a bog

after a squall
the lake rejoices
in thin
swallowey
voices

now never ends
though every second
depends

The Foot

lives at the foot

of the stairs
the mountain
the cross
the leg

foot soldiers march till they're footsore
then rest their feet on footstools

footnotes are written on poems written in feet

the fog comes on little cat feet

footmen
and footpads
hotfoot it footfirst

coltsfoot, crakefeet, drake's feet, crawfeet, crawfoot

bigfoot walks around barefoot
leaving footprints in the foothills

In youth, we have footlockers filled with footballs
(the game's afoot!)
we are footloose and fanny free,
then we take footsteps on footpaths
and find ourselves with crow's feet
and one foot in the grave

Gravediggers

for the volunteer gravediggers of the Prairie Creek
Conservation Cemetery

We offer here our labor and our time
that others may rest soundly in this place
of moss and earth and nurture. The subtle rhymes
of lift and loss in the quickly passing embrace

of shovel blade and sand reflect the gifts
of this earth we honor as we dig together or alone.
Beetles, grasses, trees, and rain and spindrift
blossoms, flesh and spirit, pass quickly along

the spinning paths all bodies follow in the arc
of time. We take our turns, we talk, and scan
the sky for birds. Soon enough it will be dark.
The cool of evening rises from the sand.

Wood Stork

I dug a grave the other day.
I helped, I mean—two others dug

as well. The soil was sandy and
the grave lay under the broad shade

of an oak. Once the hole grows deep
enough, only one shoveler

fits inside, so the others watch
and chat and then take turns. A wood

stork flew overhead as I rested.
Elegant in flight, of mournful

aspect on the ground, we call him
the Undertaker. And why,

I wonder now, do we name
the funeral director the same?

Because he literally takes
our spent bodies under the ground?

Into this cool, quiet place
I now prepare for someone else?

It smells good, this sandy earth.
I think I would happily end

my own mortal flight in this space.
Then again, the Undertaker

brings us all our babies, as we know.
And many believe the stork flies

human souls to their hereafters.
When I lie down in my final

field, I hope this genial spirit
will accompany me

on my journey, as crickets sing,
night after night after night,

their eternal, million-voiced round.

from *Empty Sleeves* (1991)

Snowy Owl

A woman who looked like a snowy owl
knocked on my door last winter.
A bunch of artificial violets was pinned
to her gray woolen coat. She trudged through the snow

in high heels, sheathed in opaque plastic boots.
Her smile was bright as a blast furnace,
and her eyes, behind double-thick glasses,
brimmed over with inspiration. "Do you,"

she began, "ever think about living forever?"
"Sometimes," I replied, staring into her yellow eyes.
She then reached in her purse and pulled out a mouse
that swung from her horny fingertips, dead.

"The gift of eternal life is not for mice.
It is for us, who know the beauty of death,
the light in the blood as it falls to earth.
Who know too the good liquor of loss,

blue terror in the fall from a great height.
Who know cruelty can be beautiful
and love a poor relation in this fine world full
of contradiction." After this she smiled

even more brightly and with great gentleness
and pride restored the dead mouse to her purse.
"Do you have any questions?" she inquired.
I thought for a moment and said, "Yes,

are you partial to a gamy cassoulet?
Perhaps I could persuade you to step in for dinner?"
She puffed out her chest and glared. The violets shivered.
She then wheeled on a sharp heel and flew away.

Swan Lake

Calling on a lady who had no maid,
I was forced to furnish my own.
In fact, I took a tea set and golden plate,
and peonies in a silver bowl.

"My word," I said to her on arriving,
"how those mourning doves do carry on!"
She peered at me most peculiarly
and ushered me into the atrium,

where scissor-tailed darts with silver spurs
and crescent wrens piped up in tandem.
She offered some crickets and Chinese tea
and we chirped through the hour most properly.

Then an odd thing transpired, direct après tea-time
(my girl had gathered the mother-of-pearl) —
my hostess, half-lidded, began to hum
a most remarkable tedium

that crept into my dangling ear-lobes,
a shell-pink delicto if I ever heard one:
"I had me a paraquat once sung so pooty
I sold my soul to a sailor-man."

I had never heard so lovely a bird-song
and fell to my knees in a reverie,
when a ruby-throated swan approached me,
duplicitous heart, amour in his eye,

a glittering black pool of romance
in which I secretly longed to swim,
so after a spot of poetic reflection,
I removed my jewels and dove in.

A Local Habitation

In November the pecans fall from their trees.
They hit the metal roof on the way down

with the sound of the tick of a wooden clock.
The nuts are brittle-shelled, full

with the wrinkled, slightly bitter meat
that smells like winter rain.

The air is a cutting blue.
When the hand reaches toward the roses,

it moves through an atmosphere
so sharp it can be felt by the skin.

Sometimes the air seems to pose
behind singular things to make them appear

even more beautiful than they are:
chrysanthemum, mockingbird, white lily.

And lulled by the slow tilt of the world's body, ghosts,
at night, daydream over fields, houses, streets,

as if a god had expelled a long-held breath
that took the shape of empty sleeves.

Apostrophe to, and Roses for, Beatrice

after Wallace Stevens

I fancied you Incarnadine,
from Early Flush to Celestial Garden.
Your flesh glows like the Tourmaline.
Your carpel charms,
my Scarlet Meillandine.

I twirled for you, my rosy queen,
your bruises too,
and your Blazing mane.
Then, heeling in your garden green,
we Carouseled,
my Ballerine.

Caprice des Dames,
my Darling Flame,
your Cuisses de Nymphe
have stormed my heaven
and veiled my sight with sensual screen.
You draped the Night,
my Crepe de Chine.

And so I knew
your metaphors.
Your Marchenland is round and blue.
Your Tristesse girdles miles and miles.
Your heart is keen.
I'll hold you
long and warm and more.
Bonne Nuit, my lovely Libertine.

Beatrice Rising

When I lived in Florida, I grew large.
It all grows large, in Florida—
the elephant ears, the cannas,
mangoes large as melons,
and the melons like Mars.
My heart ached in Florida,
large and round and stubborn,
like the moon hanging heavy
and red in the laurel oaks. My head
grew large, my eyes so large
I could see from coast to coast,
the brilliant, lonely sands,
the abrasive, shining waters.
And all those tiny houses,
hardly asleep in the night,
filled with tender nightmare
and uncontrollable desire.
And then my arms, yes my arms
grew large and began to rise
without effort, through the heavy
green night, little rivulets
of moisture slipping down my sides,
and my body too slipped slowly
from its tether, rose inch by inch
till my thighs, my knees, my calves
and ankles trickled free of the moss,
of its spidery hold. And yet
something seemed to be holding me back—
as I spun slow in the night sky

I saw with my wonderful eyes
that my heart was tangled,
ever so gently, in the feathery
ribs of the darkly draped trees.

A River of Tongues

It was dark
And getting darker,
And all the small birds
Did not call from the trees,
And generations of stones
Lay mute in the water
Which seemed
To have no history
But speculated
Over and over
On its origins.

The heavy hills looked down
In the rain, and the water
Opened its mouth
And wondered: How
Can it be that Dawn,
Wrenched nude
And chilly from her bed
Of dark feathers,
Does not tremble in the presence
Of heavy weather?
The heavy hills: She does.

And Dawn observed
How she was thrust
Again and again
Into the beginning
Of every blue day
To illuminate the ache

Of the parturition,
The formal pulse
And the deep sadness,
All the recurrent bodies
Of affection and despair, and said:

Of all the sorrows,
This was the first:
A woman came down
From her dark mountain
And offered herself
And was taken and found
She would never suffice.
But then came the children
And all the beautiful words,
And a profound tribulation
Spread through the cold, shining water.

Pungent Sauces

Fecund Regina, O queen of my lap,
I'll build a tropic temple for you—
a refulgent basilica with soaring apse
and clerestory windows. Will that do?

Here's an architrave swollen with swaying forms,
denoting the seasonable passage of time
and the watering down of all earthly devotions,
and their bitter fragrance, in pantomime.

The entablature will blaze in the gloom of night
with aromatic figures in whose magical eyes
the meaning of life will burn white on white,
reflecting the braziers of paradise.

Rosa Mistica mine, we shall figure you blessed
in a tympanum fretted with fabulous beasts—
chief among them a newt with erectile crest
and a gaggle of *pâté de foie gras* geese.

We shall feast on all feast days and give thanks to our host,
in whose monstrance lie tickets to mediate bliss.
May I savor your sauces and offer a toast
to a clement and firm metamorphosis?

De Ratione Amoris

I rest my hands
On the tablecloth.
They are hungry.

The lamp smokes.
The bread and milk
Arranged on the table
Invite the heart
Of the night
To partake.

It enters, expands.
We eat.

A silence lies under the skin.
The stars drift away from the windowpane.
It is a beautiful night.

Leaving Rome

Red poppies. White roads.
Again and again we seem to return to the real.

Through the windows
of the train the landscape

chatters in a transparent language.
See that sad green ribbon of water.

Once, it was as if a beautiful woman rose
up in violent red feathers and promised us the pure

sustained failure of a marriage of equals.
Debris in the weeds. Lengths of unlaid track.

I sometimes believe you are happy.
That is my fat, terrestrial desire.

If I could, I would live brilliantly and converse
with angels. The world pours by.

The train is full of passengers.
Hundreds of wings rushing into the dark.

Gas   after Edward Hopper

The lonely man
        performs some necessary ritual
                behind a pump. We cannot tell
exactly what it is he does because
        the angle is so odd. A rack of cans

of oil between
        two pumps on the island stands, as they do,
                conveniently available,
in easy reach of any needy
        motorist. The light is low, and the trees,

massed heavily
        behind the man and his pumps, march darkly
                off to the right. A modest shock
of roadside weeds attends the greenery
        as it condenses. On the periphery,

out of our ken,
        shines a source of artificial light. We
                are meant to feel the clutches of
evening. They are not benevolent.
        The artist has invested his talent

in loneliness.
        The values and the crusty inflections
                of his particular diction
demonstrate devotion to the modest
        fears of the soul in the longest moments

of late afternoon.
A sign hangs white above the station.
Mobilgas and Pegasus.
A flag of sorts, a standard, here, to more
than gas. The language, though hard, is clear.

Locus Amoenus

The other night I stepped
into the garden to check on the greens;
something had been eating holes in their leaves
while I slept.

There was no moon, and so
I took a flashlight and threaded my way
through the humid darkness into the rain-
soaked rows.

The broad and floppy ears
of the collards, like splayed-out cabbages,
brushed wetly against my legs as I trudged
through and peered

beneath leaves, looked over
the ground, up and down stems. In the dim light
the day's colors had faded to ash-white,
ivory,

pale green and black—the hues
of marble. I followed a wrinkled trail
through the half-light and found him—a large snail
who moved through

his corner of the dark
like a full-blown daydream, his soft body
a nimbus of flesh that seemed to study
the slow work

at hand. During the day
I had picked sleeping snails from the garden
and hurled them into the street from the yard—
a quick way

to weed them out. Their shells
crack like eggs on the pavement. I also
set out snail-bait, a cruel poison. Though
their bellies

swell up like small balloons
as soon as they eat it, it takes them hours
to die. Then the ants arrive to devour
the remains.

Yet this good night I stood
alone with the dark and peculiar grace,
the luminous flesh, the silver traces,
and I could

think only of slowly
moving caravans, distant and afoot
at dusk, the nodding pace of storybooks,
the torsos

of ancient statues. His
antennae fully extended, he took
his way through the leaves, as they lightly shook
and whispered.

Kansas Weather

She lies, they say. Embroiders her stories
and more. She is eighty-four.

Her hair is blue because out of the blue
come the blessed, bearing fruits

celestial. Without a little death
she would have nothing.

Her husband died at sixty-two.
His hands were blue

and gnarled as the bark of the cottonwood.
When she was young, when her blood

was high, crops often failed, and children died.
It was not lovely in those times.

It was blue. And duplicitous as ever. But when misfortune
undergoes a transformation

into something other than it is,
then comes the time to forgive

the tiny lapses of the natural world,
the unnatural frizz and curl

of the water parsnip, for instance.
She ponders the circumstance

of imperfection and invents, where necessary,
to save her soul. Her commentary

on the texts of things is always true.
Most clearly when the air is blue.

The Church and the Steeple

This is it.
Here is the cedar and its inhuman fruit,
the cottonwood with its many fine handkerchiefs.

Here are the ticks in their aimless procession,
their stiff-legged march through the weeds.

Here is the grave of the suicide,
set apart from the others.
If it could speak, it would tell us nothing.

This is the dust that sifts itself through its fingers.

Here is hope and a question,
an empty sleeve and a starched white collar.

This is the pallor of buds on their lonesome stems.

Here is a door.
It cannot be opened.

Here are the fields settling casually into place
and the moon that covers its tracks as it rises.

And here are two hands, folded into themselves,
a congregation, small, silent.

Now consider the palm, its particular design.
It is warm and capable and full of blood.

The Combine

Through acres of wheat
with heavy heads,
fields of hay and oats,
alfalfa, green and low,
on one of the dirt roads
that travels straight east

and west, or north
and south, curving seldom
from these straightforward
axes, over slowly rolling hills,
through an occasional pasture,
over a few curling creeks

crowded with trees,
we're driving to a shower
celebrating the engagement
of a second cousin.
The wind is blowing.
The sun is shining.

"We called him Straight Pete
Nelson," Grandmother says
from the back seat
of the car. We've passed
his old homestead,
and she's peering

out the back window
at the abandoned pile
of dressed yellow limestone
that once was a home.
"He'd stand at the ends of his rows
and stare down each one

as if his life depended
on their being straight
as blazes." Hmm. "Did you know,"
Aunt Thelma
interrupts, "that Emerald
Nyquist has taken

to drink?" "Oh, my."
The small amazement
at a world not thoroughly
correct. On the right,
the isolated but well-maintained
cemetery of the renegade

Mission devout, broken
from the Lutheran
body many years ago,
a civil war of minor
proportions. A handsome
headstone guards the Damker

plot—two large markers
and four small ones,
all the children carried off
by whooping cough
in one unspeakable stroke.
A single meadowlark

sits and preens
on a leaning post rock.
On past fields littered
with small square and big
round bales of fodder.
"Yes, they say he locked

his wife in the basement,
then prayed for her resurrection."
A pheasant trots across
an unkempt plot.
Here weeds prevail.
We change direction

at the Goldenrod
elevator, a solitary
metal structure hunkered down
beside the railroad tracks.
The complexion of the noon-
day fields is metallic—

a weather-beaten grain
glanced at by the sun.
The motion of the wheat,
in high relief and golden
as can be imagined,
is heady. Oceanic.

We fall silent, lulled
by the roll of the land, the hum
of the motor. Now, as we top
a modest rise, we see
a combine in a far field.
Harvest has begun,

and a single figure
sits high as a lookout
on his rust-colored machine,
small and angular
in the distance. Without
veering from an imaginary

line, he works his way
slowly toward the center,
guiding the stately vessel
around the selvages
of the field, felling wheat
in a wide wake behind him.

Kirkeskibe—The Ship in the Church

Denmark, Kansas

(In Denmark, as in many old seafaring countries,
it is traditional to offer hand-carved models of ships
to hang in the churches. They are given in thanks and
in praise and in hopes that the gesture will bring
good luck.)

Wind. Blows the wheat like water
and seeps under the door and curls around the feet of the pews
and stirs up some dust in the sunlight and dies in the nave.

In this heart of many hearts we know what it is
to rest light as snow on snow on a still night
and to dissolve on the tongue, on the body of an old, old love,

and we know the prayer, the dust and the ashes,
the darkened face of the prairie as it opens,
as it does and does, to receive us,

and all the small deaths in the evening,
and the blackbirds, blue and green and gold as oil
and as violet after a hard, hard rain,

and the rolling shoulders of the hills, the stone
graced thinly with its mantle of hope,
so shallow, no trees, only grass and the bitter streams.

And the ship hangs still in a quiet corner,
offering up its burden of praise,
and we know it's the same old ship of fools,
old worn, old fragile prairie schooner.

from *Green* (1998)

Bricolage

My eyes are on the blink again, so I stagger around the kitchen
pottering with the bric-a-brac and trying to see through these roiling

and apparently imaginary chains that look like black-and-white DNA
    strands
inside my eyeballs and thinking, well,

at least I'm not writing mournful wise poems of rare lyrical
    attentiveness,
when all of a sudden I think of you and your bedroom eyes.

"Romance is my life," I wish I could say, but I can't, Lesley Blanch
has already said it so I think I'll leave *that* one lay where Jesus flang it

and focus my fraying attention on The Wilder Shores of the cupboards
and cleaning under the toaster, the sort of thing one can accomplish

while deep blue pools expand and contract and obscure the immediate
    and present
in one's range of vision. The great thing about *seeing* is its infinite
    variety

and the fact that it can be managed under almost any condition, even in
    the dark.
For instance, I can see you very clearly now, your long tall frame,

the shine of those little lights on the cool wet pavement,
the dark and tender neighborhood we inhabited for a time.

Another Passionless Day

Nel mezzo del camin what one finds is beans
and wrinkled cabbage and an awful case
of ambling vacuity, an affliction resembling

walking pneumonia, but worse in its long-winded
and peevish consequences, so one shuffles and pokes
through jars of ointment and old hockey pucks

tucked away in the armoire to find just exactly
the right sort of eyewash or what is left
of one's former, nobly galloping convictions,

but what one discovers, among the stoppered monuments
to ancient prostrations, is a B-flat clarinet
and a parched umbrella, so one decides

with waffling confidence to put on some weight
and to belly up to some giant pastries
in a health-food bar where one is likely

to meditate, darkly, on the gnarled knobble
of *the rich tapestry of life* whereupon one decides
one is finally embarrassed by one's youthful enravishments

and regrettably public declarations of enthusiasm
for items no longer in one's possession,
and at this point one wonders if it might not be wise

to camp out from now on on a platform that features
some zazen sitting and banana smoothies,
when *mirabile dictu* one is relieved to realize,

as one waddles out fatly to the tattered edge
of old *terra firma*, that the fruits of one's labors
are likely to grow more textured and complex

the plumper and softer the bottomland,
so one stands on the strand of the continent,
at the prow of the knowable with a valiant pulse

and a homemade sandwich and peers, ever hopeful,
at the roiling sea of contradictions
that presses in on the beaten sand.

In the Library

A warbling shaft of sunlight enlightened
my carrel at the doleful end of the other day

as I sat there idling, no petulance in sight,
admiring my sublime and shattering nails

when this perfect peace comes walloping in
through the window and smears a fine Phoenecian

radiance all over the surfaces of Life.
Beneath it all hummed a giant vacancy,

a mindset that harbors no idiot foibles—
no slogging through the whanging tracts

of Romance, for example, no earaches, no pimples,
no hopeful, standard, blurry vision.

A pure pacific entertainment
weighed into the scheme of things beneath

the mansard roofs of higher education
and I felt for a hefty and eternal minute

like a strongman bearing up with splendid fortitude
beneath the unbearable barbells of bliss.

"Trapped in my rib-cage something throes and aches!"

John Berryman

This flu was weird, delightfulness and perishing,
a hot surprise in a chilly sandwich.

The germ inhaled transfigured things, put wings
on cells and brought the local crew to riot,

to gaily filch from daily routine welter
the many measured certainties of self.

A breach of borders, edges, frame—invasion
with a loss of breath, a wandering, wayward thing.

Ambivalent, it rained on thermal pools
and the parched departments, then gathered up its arsenal:

arrows, fire-tipped and plain; fever; boxing gloves & bits;
animals (wild) and stinging bees; biting, piercing congeries—

and then it left. And left me fresh
and wondering at the wantonness of flesh.

Premature Ventricular Contractions

My heart, my heart, my interrupted heart—
it leaps when it should lie in bed, inert
and primly decent. It carries on, apart
from the silent embrace of its short-
sighted, tired corpus, and fibrillates—
tails of nervous fish in a deep dark flirt.

Alcaic Figure

I'm sweating. Tossing. Sleep is impossible.
Damn blankets. Ankles caught in the undertow.
    Hot breath of attentive mosquitoes. A swelling of
    doubt and the whining of tiny woodwinds.

Bad day. I didn't do it the way that I
should have. This heat is brazen. I think of my
    two beautiful daughters. I'm never the mother I
    want to be. Barking. It sounds like oboes.

No. Horns. I could get up and continue to
read *Death in Rome*. I won't. All the characters
    repel me. I'm breathing the one thousand two thousand
    three thousand laurel tree where the hell is

that dog? There's sand awash in the bed sheets, I
hold off the weight, the terrible slowness of
    tides. Nine thousand ten I am sinking now, classical,
    shifting impurities, reedy, stranded.

Pale waves, the sea is scrambling to climb up the
beach, foaming notes, like Morpheus muttering—
    shades, white and sublunary, washing ashore to those
    masses of children with pale blue faces.

Dog Sonnet

(by Gracie)

I know where I'm going
Plutarch's coming with
Off to goof drobble sproing
Snoop a rich double whiff
Fish kill at the sinkhole
O magnificent luck
Grabble pute marly roll
In the turrible druck
Hey a mole wholly rapture
Dig it four paw full blown
Wait a minute got fleas
Got to stickle the flap
Of this ear here's a bone
Prone to me. Sneeze.

Byzantium

Early summer, Istanbul.
The light is green and sweet and pale;

dark ferries slice the morning's veils.
On leafy Greengrocer Bayram street

hunch mountains made of artichokes.
Fish shine in rings on blazing trays

and the volume of the vendors' calls
gains weight as traffic circulates.

Copper is shaped with rhythmic strokes
in crabbed streets where in older days

the golden insects of Apollonius
sang like brazen parakeets.

*

A literary critic flew
to Istanbul, once, to pursue

some literary notions *re:*
the rectitude of Constantine,

the triumph of the western line.
The cocksure fellow never sailed

the ferries that continue to cross
the waters of the Bosphorus;

he had a headache, I believe.
He dreamed a nightmare, then pronounced

all of Asia squat and foul
and rode his line straight out of town

to calm his nerves in Athens, Greece.
He missed the boat entirely.

*

East and west, the interplay
of form and soul, of gold and dark,

of Greek and of the Abbassid,
the Persian and the Byzantine,

find incessant synthesis
on the shoulders of the Bosphorus

whose water serves to both unite
and separate two continents,

as autumn runs and shines between
the banks of heat and winter's scrim.

*

Snow on the ground. Heavy and wet.
Sheets of light shroud hulking mosques.

Ferries now glide in and out
of blinding fog with two lights, grim,

ablaze on each black, dreaming mast.
Soul here sails the what-has-been,

its contrast and complexity,
shifting images that correspond

to starlit domes of heirarchs,
to tankers in the churning sea.

Dolphins in the Snow

Lines and sheets of white are blown, light conjugations,
in layered, flustered carousels and large

and hissing plates that skim and feint and charge
the pewter, mildly rolling scintillation

of the surface. Dolphins punctuate
the veneer, their dorsal fins appearing slow

and smooth, in cursive, off the starboard bow.
The light is thin and perishing and late.

These incomparable wandering voices, these gray
and graceful constructs of another language

correspond in gloss, and passengers surround
the rails to scan the ample waterway

for signs, for the filaments of lineage
to something resonant, fluent, and profound.

Drinking Wine on a Hill Above the Confluence of the Bosphorus and the Golden Horn

for Jane Morse

High above the congregation of the laminated waters,
muscular and clear, that deeply and to great

effect reverse themselves in diurnal, layered turnings,
that lap between the Marmara, a heaving marble sea,

and the glassy Euxine, twice a day, at least,
the "cow ford," Io's refuge from the torment of the fly,

the Bosphorus, the blue veneer that "with one key,"
says Gyllius, "opens and closes two worlds, two seas,"

and the black and stinking Golden Horn, where sludge
flourishes in sun, where black enamels all the piers

and boats and anchor ropes, where potent Ottoman fleets
once harbored, *Chrysokeras* (O gilded name), where subterfuge

bubbled up in darkness more than once to author
the splendid fall of fabled empire—up here, at night,

one scans the expanse of civil lights to try to see
what lies beneath the sheets, the film, the fine

and stratified detritus of significant events
to refine the figures, exfoliate the press of things,

to clarify the confluence of vessel and vexation
as ferries skim the surfaces, as drops slip down the glass.

Cow Ford

Io driven in heat by imperishable hardscrabble frantic desire
    unstoppered and heftily stumbling cowfooted wild and
    lowing across many lands finds her way to this water
    and wobbles in

It cools her a while as she fords and leaves behind floating a
    whispery foam filling the folds of the deep green shoreline
    her fame and her station a hint of a soothing in language
    that conjures her scalding flight

She flies from the west to the great flashing east and then
    wheels around under to fall to her knees on the banks of
    the Nile where finally Hera relents and releases the
    incandescent hand from her sex

And now from the north to the south and the south to the north
    at a slow and majestically sensual pace great tankers
    bear down on the deep shifting currents to service
    economies far from home

Marriage: A Moment

Comes back, comes back the trouble, days can pass
and months then *wham* the nasty neverending
wham — there's not enough there's too much raving
impulse slams the oiled machine (my ruby ass)
transgression's pure disequilibrium,
distress undressed, O need to need,
(*amo, amas*) O dithyrambic, pedigreed-
with-DNA-embossed imperium
Oh I'm OK Oh no you're not and while
we're at it where the fuck's the very ground
on which this edifice (baroque)'s supposed
to stand? It's heaving and the herm's defiled —
it's smashed in tiny, momentary mounds
of plasma. Damn. Let's metempsychose.

For My Mother

At the time of your long dying you touched
with your clumsy hand the firm white body
of my baby your skin so fragile it wept
and your eyes bright and wet as the scales of a fish
My little white whale you called her your language

richer in metaphor the thinner your grasp
on us as you swelled in the white trunk
of redundant flesh that spread in your bed
as you died We spoke on the phone
and you wandered—a visit to me in Oklahoma

you said *such a nice visit*—and then you were gone
and I was fiercely glad for you no more pain no more overflowing
vessels no more unbearable weight And the moon
has filled now many times and the glaze on my eyes
comes and goes and sometimes the mornings are heavy

The baby is two and gives us great joy but I need
to know where you have gone—is it off in the waters
or bright and permanent in the sky?
your body is now ash and in the dirt
but I need to know do you correspond

with the stony mass of the spheres? do you rock
in some dark grand basin lapping the shores
of the light and the tangible? do we breathe
you in with the air? do you still swell with love
to the drum of her small, splendid heart?

Shore

Drenched in the light and seduced by the brilliant green lie of the duckweed,
my two-year-old daughter steps off the low dock and onto the fabulous
figment of landscape composed by a million small fraudulent islands.

A tissue of green and brown granules draws over her head in a second.
The islets, up-ended, reveal their unearthly and frayed isolations
to me as I throw myself down to the false ground that has swallowed my baby.

My hand rends the fabric's insidious surface—I'm numb and I'm blind
as I palpate the darkness, my fingertips brushing what feels like fine filaments—
softest of cilia, gossamer algae. Unlike the unfortunate

Demeter, I am granted the gift of my daughter, unharmed and indignant,
covered in duckweed, insulted by water and the tug on her hair
that drew her up over the glistening fringe of the splintery dock.

Rain

It so happens I'm tired of desire,
of the mouths of the thousand things endlessly calling,
of the tongues of lemons, the voices of men,
the taste of iron and salty linen.
It so happens I'm tired of the pulling,
the vigorous dance of the charming ego,
the songs of the kitchen, the boiling sonata,
bite of the tweezers, the plumbing's whine.
I'm tired of passion, counterfeit or otherwise,
tired of prices, of heft and of gain,
of the towering columns, the whole archipelago
of plummeting bridgework and dangerous vines.
I want to lie down and transmogrify sentences,
I want to dissolve on a cool gray cloud.
When the sky bends down to pleasure the ground,
the rain is cool; it's dark and it rains.

Green

Storms in the east
lightning over the hill

west of the stone
stoop the light

is green, green
as new wine

and smooth and soft
and slightly threatening

it bathes the body
of the parched yard

wetting the leaves
of the trees and the stiff

dry grass, green
all the way to the creek

green as a snake
in the trees, green

as going, as water
in so many poses

over pebbles
and sand

around things
that hesitate

and mossed roots
green as what was

and how one felt
green as a question mark

green as cheat
green as the calm

before catastrophe

from *From Istanbul / İstanbul'dan*
(1998)

Termessos

From ashlar blocks cool to the hand
    from the passionately accurate spaces between them
from cisterns brimming with desiccated comment
    from the heard but invisible snake in the brush
rise the word walls of a ruined city

Wait they seem to be saying *wait*
    they have waited through mountainous declensions of time
through bronze panels of sunlight that transfigure the fall
    and lisping snows and the engorgements of spring
Wait they say in the dialect of stones

that converses with surge and the moving earth
    there is work to be done there are cores to mine
there is a future here of geometrical purity
    if you just take the time to analyze the lines
and to scrape and examine the speech-pocked friezes

Wait they repeat and I navigate a cleft
    with the feet and the heart and the desire to believe
in this stone-born imperative and its constellations of lichen
    that testify there is no last diminishing
there is only the organic work of translation

from *Celestial Bodies* (2002)

Mouth-River

I want to raise some notes from the under-mind
and fan the rumors at bed-time
the beautiful word-fall that churns up from a ripe center

I want I want I want
rises from the fire diaphragm
laps on the shores of the throat and rides out on the tongue

tête et amour
immensity and pleasure-dew
are better than a bank full of pretty money

there's enough beauty in this world to choke a god

Chin Song

Let me confess:
    in this prefabricated world,
        in among the 10 million replacement parts,

I am a creature of the comforts of sin.
    I like sitting on the golden fence
        that cleanly bisects the Problem Swamp.

I like a bracing game of metaphor roulette.
    On the odd, fluid, and unlit occasion,
        I indulge in an act of passionate reading.

In this province where happenstance is a major occurrence,
    I frequent the do-wop bar.
        I go dancing with my beloved at The Listening Jam

and get hot feet.
    Then we sit high on the banks of the Late Fall River
        and feel coolly debauched.

But I have great intestinal fortitude
    and rarely require the Paregoric of Life,
        so don't worry about me.

See that low purple cloud,
    that smear on the horizon?
        That's where I'll make my fabulous fortune.

Un Messaggio per il Corpo

I'm busting out of this seraglio.
There are hot strawberries out west,
and I want a childish million.
I'll go pound the ponderosa
with a nobotnik or an errant male
to help undefine the moment.
This is known as the buddy-ro system.
We'll be in a large constructivist pique,
which is really a ponderosity,
but we'll make stunning progress.
We'll locate the Lakota Dharma
and slip into a vast energy warehouse.
We'll watch the eerie transfigurations
in the winter sunrise, and then we'll waltz.
Then we will disinherit the earth.
It will have been a stewy tempus.
An absolutely magnificent failure.
What a wonderful waste.
I love this phase.

Ideology Stinks, But the Heart Smells Pure

I'd been living for years with an adolescent boy,
investing in yachts and party suits, that sort of thing,
when a real convergence struck me:
where there is scarcity in the boudoir

and malevolence in the pit of the stomach,
it's time to do the disappearing unit.
I did.
I belted in my eyeballs,

did some marginal hoofing,
and leaped off a nearby precipice.
I sailed by the relics of an overblown landscape
until I stumbled onto Happenstance College.

This is what I saw:
an abstract god lounging on the lawn on a starry blanket.
Sometimes he got up to paint on no apparent easel.
He pondered the question of the Happiness Game

and decided it couldn't be renewed.
This was an anorectic rex, I decided,
not much interested in radicalization of the spirit.
So I moved on.

Clutching my small, heartfelt purse,
I headed for the mirrored academy
to study the politics of exile and engagement.
Here, in the absence of desire,

I realized at once that the dervish of my soul
ached with more thought than usual,
and so I moved on once more.
A fever of angels assailed me and spoke:

show your bare feet and we'll negotiate.
So I did and they did,
and after some enormous lunch dates on Sundays
I began to smell optimism in the nearsomeness

of genuine mouth-to-mouth intelligence.
I understood now how the hand of desire
will always reach for the purple heart-candy
and that, most of all, this is a miracle of design.

And that perfection is basically mild.
So now we can examine my many disenthornments
and have some romantic fruitcake.
Come on over here and join me, you mild slickered bird.

Approaching Fifty

> I'm not doing any of that croning shit,
> I can tell you right now.—Donna M.

I've graduated from behavioral college.
I've met my share of cataclysmic goof-balls.
I've been wheeled in to the emergency era
and introduced to the triumph report.
Insurance enablers line the highway to disaster,
where I'm leaning now on a motionless stick.
I'm looking for the great high words,
but what comes are *mumblety-peg* and *washing machine*.
I smell a crude ruined smell.
It's a slice of wince pie.
I am handed some academic pliers
by a man with a too-proud expression on his face.
It's a kind of lesion.
He asks me to manufacture, out of all this,
an argument for stellar equality.
OK. Give me the materials and don't make me pant.
It isn't so simple. It's an amazement.

Out for a Walk

My soul took itself out for a walk the other day
It hasn't yet returned and I'm slightly concerned

it used to say it always wanted to travel the world
it used to say it couldn't help it if its essence was larger than the room
in which we lived
it used to say it's terrible how it longed to converse with other flesh

So what should I do?

should I allow myself the rich dark honey of a jealous rage?
should I breathe slowly and count to ten thousand several hundred
times?
should I harrow the black soil of my body for clues?

Perhaps I'll just sit quietly and swing my foot
Perhaps I'll just listen to this fatal thudding in my chest

Ars Longa

I

Why must art
be long, I ask?
Why not sizzle
up the task?
Largo, says
the rhapsodist,
snappy hands
make counterfeits.

II

Latefall light
in Florida—
intimate gold
camera.
Moistly dying
overtones
muscled up
in little bones.

III

Vita brevis,
this is why
soul lives in
an open eye,
swallowing
in hopeful bits
morsels
of the infinite.

Time Is Money

Gray nickels up
in the east—

the forecast
is dire, but

it is a stately sight.
Dogs are whirping

at the moon in China
and a string quartet

has rattled out
an ardent arabesque

that brings consumers
to their knees.

Here is a common heresy:
Things are Bleak.

See here—this bag
of olives on my lap

is radiating happily
its currency.

Let's slurp it up
in unison

and celebrate
inflation for a change.

And racket.
Let's celebrate as well

that quarter
where wind smells

like wet steel
and the children

laugh unshod and holler
through their hands.

Where epistemology
is chocolate

and bags of olives
mean a lot.

Where power of attorney
counts for nothing.

Where time is racing
through the sluicegates,

every second
riotous in diamonds.

This world is burning
up in beauty.

Time and a Dog

All right we can't repeat the past
don't want to bones are in the grass
time and a dog regard them mildly
sniff and pass on to other piles
what's round the bend is *entre nous*
mon ancien amour, mon âme I'm through
with *dies irae* through with twirping
on about the mess the bird
has turned the dog has yapped the heart
has swollen in the cage and partly
mooned it's almost full it's time
to wash the hands and look sublime

Sundog to Moondog

You teach and sing, my friend.
I think that's why you need a drink.
You got one foot in the sublime, the other prinked
in acrobatic shoes. C'mon pal, lose
the stuffy props. It's time you whapped your tail
in time to some rhapsodic blues.

OK then son, I lift my glass of palest ale.
A toast to bluest rhetoric, a toast to stumpy you.

Ah, misery, my friend, is grand, if threaded very fine.
A heart in hanker heated up is sweet and unbenign.

And unbeknownst to us.

Ah, yes.
Would wunst upon a time the gods could jimmy ope
the hole that keeps celestial types a million years,
in light, apart, and, yes, I fear,
a-mope.

Pluteus Petasatus

Night. A mute white dwarf
in earthmoving hat
bulbs up from the mold.

It has nudged and shoved
its smart headstrong head
through the discrete wood.

Now its exquisite
fruiting body feeds
on the broke-down else,

infiltrates the blank
detritus of lives,
and rises and smells

like a star. This is
degenerate news,
the small moonlit kind.

Chimaera   Yanartaş, Turkey

The beastly hot flesh
    of the beach's nude white sand
        sears the feet even

in the dark the waves
    a quiet lace ornament
        on hissing water

from here we climb up
    the mountain's flank it's hairless
        and strange and arid

pebbles chuckle down
    the trail is thin my flashlight
        flashes and ranges

like a wild white
    chicken no moon hot darkness
        radiating down

aqueous lightnings
    prick at the backs of the eyes
        here is the odor

of seeping gases
    here is the face of the beast
        small fires in the ground

little blue tongues cold
    to the eye lap formally
        at the night's profile

*

I've stalked my way here
    to this mythical minute
        on the creature's lip

down a metaphorical path
    whose wobbly complex of wrong
        destructive pieces

and powerful beauties
    resembles this old
        monster grappled up

by sailors heaving
    on the ragged growling breast
        of an ancient sea

and now here I am
    scrambling over the stone face
        peering down into

the hot compound eyes
    and wondering from the outskirts
        of the fractured ground

if a tangle with
    the handsome Bellerophon
        on his magical steed

with the great
    and poetic wings isn't just
        what I really need

Dancing at the *Binbir Gece*

Istanbul

We've bluefished, wined, succinctly smoked and drunk
of course too much and now my queer friend J
and I stroll arm in woolen arm the nightfell
streets. In words as fine as feathers I
contend our other queer friend P who strolls
in rings of light before us is an angel.
J waves and snorts and says but he's my dear
a dedicated homo-seck-syu-all,
and thus we sail the fairly stable streets
to the delinquent doors of *Binbir*, a low
delighted bar, which hugely swells
with many beauteous creatures, some not so,
all ample in their finery, but first
I think I'll pee. I amble into the ladies'
and pull up stumped to see a handsome man
darken his eyes in the mirror as I've forgotten
where I am, if I ever really knew.
I turn to go but Sloe-eyes reels me back.
Oh come on in we're all girls here, and yes,
of course, I think and then I enter, flush,
depart the stall and find that in that shuttered
moment more have bloomed upon the sink.
We chatter and prink and rattle on—mascara,
blush, and men, and when they ask and I
say poet then this pressing issue hungers
up with striking eyes—do I write of *passion?*
And yes I say of course and we all soar
at this intelligence and float out on a sea
of joy, I to my angel and our earthly companion,

they to their feathery poetic evening quest
and from this black box in the night I believe I can see
how common and beautiful is the secret best
we all compose to take our next light steps.

from *Stroke* (2007)

No Comfort to be Had

After it happened, the blood pressure soared.
Half the body wept, one hand on its brow,
while one of its two legs began to march
to the drum of that which had prevailed.
One half of the brain, bewildered, racked itself
in search of comfort, while the other, firmer
half scoured the mall for a gown for the ball.

The body, thus arrayed in perfect discord,
one foot crammed in a party shoe, now
began to stagger around the room, starched
and wilted all at once. One eye, the pale
one, stared at the clock ticking on the shelf
whose face concealed a belly full of worms.
One hand nailed the orders to the wall.

Deep Gossip

I

Concerto grosso, blackest heart,
A mystifying natal chart—
All ignite the metaphoric art.

II

A planetful of pure desire
Is all a poet should require
To set the commonplace afire.

III

The heart that hides inside the form
Observes the words that fume and swarm:
No one lives above the storm.

Insurance

I'm recklessly flying
my wind-sheared bicycle
no sun-screen no cell phone

I'm loose on the sun-drowned
prairie and chirping *Look
Ma no goddamned helmet*

and Ma at this moment
is standing her fragile-
boned crooked old frame as

straight as she can on the
ledge of her stair-chair and
pushing the button and

rising like a goddess
from the dark undertow
borne upward on a shell

yet bound of course to fall
and it's clear that we need
a policy for when

imagination fails
when an ocean of fact
and white foaming despair

rushes up the hard legs
and submerges the heart
of the head-strong rider

when the tangy salt smell
disaster brings powders
our transported bodies

and threatens our moving
and most always precise
navigations which are

full of prolific doubt
but dazzlingly feathered
and fabulously real

The Visionary from Apopka

had faith in the largesse of the living
but carried with him
a dozen hand-made urns,
just in case.

He had been born
in a church bathroom
and therefore had a practical habit of mind.
He often organized madrigals at sunset.

I'd had a scuffle with a woman
who had *monkey* written all over her
and needed some compound word-matter
to settle my nerves.

How do hew do? I inquired
and he forgave me and gave me his shoes.
You're just in time for the squirm-fest, friend,
he said. *You may also wash your feet.*

I didn't have a forever grant,
but we dealt with that as masterful adults.
We approached the ultimate adding machine
and grabbed us a statue bereft of sin

and some mausoleum gear.
There's not enough shriek and swagger
in our utterly transgressive faith, he confessed,
but he looked down on the others

in their cold, crawling context.
Those people are injured by the time of day,
he sniffed. As we entered a carnelian cloud,
I suggested we leave early and often.

All's well that ends in the dirt, he said.

The Body Politic

Evil thrives in a variety of plumages;
in protruberant behavior, in brief deceits.

We wander its corridors on the cusp of business,
a mighty fabric over the eyes,

our private darknesses illumined by paraffinalia
and its non-combustible flame,

while the lesser profondeurs blandish and surl
in a controlled burn. It's all map and no shingle.

It's wickedness on fire with bodily intent.
Grotesqueries with a huge probability of failure.

An adroit robbing style with a beau regard.
Rotundity and crenellation.

So their trembling emissary is in a royal jam,
says *get out the way and lissen—*

an apparition at the gate will very soon cast a glance
over your sodden company.

Under that cool cloud over there is a fuming trope,
but it's for the brethren only. And the deputy steppers.

What we are left with is the quantity racket,
muffled illusions and a very great sadness.

We are dazed and in the open,
on our way to the foreghastly conclusion.

Time's List of Things To Do

Time wants to write a poem
about the metaphorical mind
but first has to fiddle in a pocket
for a pencil.
Outside the window
trees are inching upward
in graceful green increments.
Time is seized by a sense of duty
and writes, inspired:
     soup
     sigma
     soap froth
     delta
     volcano
     error
     tau
     then
     smiles
     and
     gently
     wears
     the
     pencil
     down.

The Vulgate of Experience

In this tatterdemalion sandwich of Life,
it pays to pay attention to the light,

not to the oligarchic spread of heavy principles,
or to four-week traditions.

There are multitudes caught in the glare
and just as many stuck in a radiant head-book.

The book says even though we might reflect
the bruised glory of all the suns

that ever shone down on the earth,
mostly everyone's dreaming in a savage room

or searching for the beloved in the desert.
I admit I, for one, am clouded by experience,

though I'm feeling my way into a weird pre-waking
from the old parabola of darkness.

Some nights I sleep in wild weather
where the names of the gods change furiously.

Sometimes I wander in the available light.
The wind is always a perilous distraction.

On rare, sweet days I hear a brown, nut-like sound.
Inside this sound you can hear the imagination fluttering.

Here joy whiskers through the main arteries.

Here is where, if you hold out your hands, they will be filled.

Four Tiny Sonnets

*

I

After the Flood, Frogs

assemble,
whirp
and
fart,
dissemble,
delve,
and
throng,
prolonging
the
agglutinant
song
of
themselves

II

Pity the Poor Orange

bald
white
orb

on
the
table
rests

its
veined
membrane
exposed

flayed
for
zest

III
Adam and the Snake Prepare to Recite Some Verse

Snake
says

let's
go
mezmerize
some
pomes

Adam
says

I
prefer
to
mammarize
them

IV
Corrective

Sorry,
but
nature's
first
green
is
red,

in
spite
of
what
Mister
Frost
said.

Gold
arrives
later
in
willow
and
birch.
Red,
like
blood,
runs

last
and
first.

*

Driving to Assos

As the road drops
    down from
        the mountains

west of Balıkesir
    and passes
        through Edremit

it turns floral
    coastal
        delicious

the countryside
    is olive-groved
        and gracious

the roadside
    lavishly dressed
        in sunflower

wild hollyhock
    blue and martial
        thistle in windy

light and everywhere
    the radiant blood
        of poppies

the olive trees
    tended and hacked
        as appears

to be necessary
    crouch venerable
        and gray

in the stony
    old groves
        on the shore

      *

Brown towns
    along the way
        are frilled

in roof-high roses
    and hollyhocks spill
        over sidewalks

and farther on
    a holiday village
        simmers in the heat

under a mantle
    of dust and here
        is Kücükküyü

at the countryside's
    ragged edge
        the hillsides far

more bouldery
    than before
        now the road

climbs the hill
    behind Behramkale
        and reaches

the top and the sky
    opens out
        the earth falls

away beneath
    the feet and
        far below green-eyed

Lesbos lazes
    in the hazy
        shimmer of the sea

            *

High among the ruins
    above the shore
        the air bristles

in the thrill of lemon
    thyme and sage
        I am quite alone

except for a herd
    of belled sheep
        tinking and bonging

over the Roman road
    meandering up
        from the sea

here
    in the middle way
        the sun spills

in great sheets
    into the agora
        a slight rustle

betrays a snake
    gliding across
        the trail

it's mythical
    and still
        this golden

earth-bound spirit
    observes me
        with quiet eyes

then whips
    away through
        the brush

and a moment
    later flows back
        across the sun-stroked path

a liquid omen
    in which I rinse
        all the force

of my manifold
    desires and
        quite

suddenly
    the texture
        of the instant opens

the frame
    it saturates
        the borders

and the light
    of all that's possible
        burns through

Hystericalectomy

Yesterday's tulips in the crystal bowl
have begun to open and already they've
partially exposed their pistils and stamens.
In the coming days
these petals will open in a brazen
yawn, their private parts thrust
into the shocked and fascinated
room. Very soon the whole
apartment will start to misbehave—
the fainting couch and ottoman will shed their raiment,
weirdness will graze the ceiling and raise
eyebrows in the carpet lice. With sex emblazoned
on the air, the afflicted chamber will swell with lust.
A hystericalectomy is clearly indicated.

Drought

In the dessicated lies the windy ones thunder,
in the heat of each day more concentrated in dismay

than the last, while fanatics fan the daily burn
and the social contract withers in disarray,

the dog days dog and the hollow nights fall.
I am helpless to stop them. Instead I sprawl

in this pool of glossy words. They are all I have
to irrigate our green and fluent mundo.

Avant-gardening on my weeping knees

tending to the green
immargination of the plot

I tidy up the loose ends of my lines
while all about me twine

the scrollwork and fretwork
of intelligent and perverse design

wing-stroke and piston-stroke
play heartburn music

on the underside of sense
while I pursue

the noble and miserable hounds
of vernacular economics

turning over spadefuls of apparent earth
my fat and vocable wealth

the soil here is the soul
of intelligence

a miracle of steadfastness
in the windy mess

that splatters the whole as I range widely
and with complicated passion

in the dirty possibilities
of the fascinating ground

Little Pirate Song

We feeled icky. Words
abuzzed in the sticky air.

The blue profondeur reeled and was rolly.
To a man, we resolved to the stalwart flair,

but instead, we fell toothless.
Toothless and ruthless.

Out on the mezzo-poop deck we admired them sail:
magnificent frigate birds.

Grand Disastery

moored by fine
tethers to certain death

a hornet fizzes
on the windowsill

a spider flies
to its side

to securely bind
this abundant harvest

the hornet in shrill
thrall to agony drills

a hole in God's
improvident breast

pocket
in the sublime

cold light
of this tiny

constellation
the bald pulp

of the hornet's diminishing
hum feeds growing eyes

and hungry sockets
the figure is clean

a small
black aster

hung among
the stars

A Computerized Jet Fountain in the Detroit Metro Airport

I.M. Richard Wilbur

Perfect tubes of water,
shot from hidden modern grottoes, their flat
cylinder heads drily intact,
leap and curve, swift and sleek as otters

and equally alive,
as if they sported minds of their own and knew
exactly where they had to get to
and when. Their muscularly perfect dive

into the flat, shining
mirror of the surface that receives them
is a miracle of theorem,
mathematical and clean, at once defining

joy and pure control.
The parabolic arches made of time
and pressure express the delicious rhyme
of flight and landing, melting in the bowl

of sure return, the end
its own beginning. The fullness of desire
frolics here in fluid attire
and recognizes, even as it bends

in play, the underside
of bliss, in polished granite, adamant and black.
We travelers will end up back
where we began, so may our gods provide

us all with equal grace
and fluent spirit on our way, even
if our paths won't chart the heaven
towards which all hungers leap, all pleasures race.

from *Straits & Narrows* (2013)

Animist Manifesto

where is God
we ask in haste

and answer slow
in winter-paced

adagio:
in appetite

in thrum
and fissure

in pressure
in the deep-set

vein in silence and
in marbled sleep

in the garbled dream
of working men

with far-flung
shoulders in

the steady hum
of axled tires

in their endless
turning and

the slow burn
of their prose

in the autumn
poetics of fire

in the mordant
tones of blazery

in fall-stroked
polyphonic meadows

in the darkness
of the Dorian scale

the shadowed face
and tangled dance

that trails
all music

and its fragrance
in the winding

sonnetude
of grief

that punctures
every day's veneer

in all bodies bound
by gravity

in the splendor
of the soul-fish

floating in
their water holes

waiting patiently
for amplitude

for metaphor
for the song

of mind
made flesh

Boulder

this world
is full

of beautiful
surprises

here's one:
one bright

blue noon
on Loon

Lake I sat
on the porch

eating lunch
and watched

a chipmunk
on the compost

pile nibble
a strand

of spaghetti
until he'd

consumed
it all and then

I heard
a tremendous

fluster
in the lake

a moose
had quietly

been munching
on underwater

plants—fine
delicacies

to northern
ruminant types

and what
I had taken

to be a boulder
turned out

to have been
her shoulder

as her submerged
mouth hoovered

up all the juicy
stems of my water

lilies until
her hungry

lungs ached
for air

and she reared
her head

in a great
splendor

of bright water
a sloshing

slurping
slurry

of mud
and stems

profuse and
dripping

from her
streaming

maw as she
observed

me coolly
before

heading down
for more

Interlude

the never-ending
meditation

continues in
this early

morning
squirrels on

the porch
and in the trees

the lake is still
the silence

blue I've belled
the cat made

coffee and
am ready

with my pencil
to accept

whatever
mind imagines

is its music
or its body

or its gold
I've hung

the niger
thistle-seed

and am
waiting

for the cloud
of goldfinches

I hear is near
to appear.

Such Luck

in the larger
darknesses

of the ground
west of sight

I'm shouting
at the mountain

of silence
and depth

when
an eye opens

and I open
my mouth

to devour
the sound

of night
which in time

will filter
through all

that swings
or hums

my fist
is full

of letters
my wrist

aches like
a drum

such luck
to hold

this compendium
of resonant

voices in
the sanatorium

of my head
whose guest-

book is
crowded

with the high-
brow and

the low-brow
and whose

overseer
in the back-

ground prays
every day

for my bright
daughters

and the black
blue waters

they're swimming
through and all

the possibilities
they might

swallow
and I know

my strength
and sphere

may be slight
but look

at this
handful

of light
I found

in a crack
in the ground

here
it's for you

In the Mood for Love

Evening falls
onto the shoulders

of the trees
across the lake

the quiet air
wants me to be

out in it
but I remain

inside watching
a Chinese

movie *In
the Mood*

for Love
and now

my lover
calls from

the city and we
reimmerse

in the slow
dark warmth

of our recent
meeting and

now the lake
too is calling

to me I want
intensely

to soak
in that light

right now
and it occurs

to me a finite
amount

of golden
light

remains
to my life

as the red
squirrels

quarrel
on the porch

and I return
to the Chinese

movie which
concerns

adulterous
lovers

and naturally I
think of my own

adulterous
lover and see

again the fireflies
that lazily

surprised us
in the dusk

of the park
and the haze

of our accustomed
pleasures

or should I say
understandings

and now some
children kayak

by in their
red and yellow

boats and their
calls and laughter

return me to
an evening

long ago on
this same lake

I'm rowing with
a handsome young

philosopher and we're
one of a phalanx

of boats heading
to the western edge

of the lake in search
of a diabetic

boy lost
in the darkening

marsh and
the philosopher

and I are
ferrying

the game warden
whose body

odor powerful
as a corpse in heat

wafts back and chokes
us sniggling

at the oars
but he was the one

who found
the boy in

the impossibly
mosquitoed

northern swamp
and brought

him back and
now I'm back

to the movie
where a very

long moment
is devoted

to the smoke
that sensually

envelops
the handsome

lead and I
remember

the *Bodies*
exhibit we saw

in Tampa
where the flayed

and disemboweled
corpses of many

Chinese dead
were mounted

and posed
to instruct our

healthy western
children on

the intricate beauty
of the inner self

and we all
clearly saw

that all these
exposed lungs

were charcoal
black and

now night has
truly fallen

the wind
has dropped and

the life-jacketed children
call to their life-jacketed

parents and
paddle home

and in the Chinese
movie it sounds

like Nat King Cole
is crooning in

slightly
awkward

Spanish to us all
as the sexy

smoke swirls
around the head

of the sexy
married man

and so much is lost
in the translation.

Form

and now the lake's
slate-gray

the trees
a green fringe

and deeper
in the distance

the mountain
hulks and presses

its blue form
insistently

on the eye
absolutely

everything
at stake

at every
moment

Prairie

everything
shines

the water
the grasses

sun and wind
and alligators

on the move
in the sink

moorhens
chuckle

and bleat
as the wings

of the boat-
tailed grackle

whoosh
and he purple

and royal blue
and green passes

through
this beautiful

high system
each creature

here pursues
another and

the beating
flailing thing

fights down
the gullet

to become
the shine on

another's wing
I wish

for equanimity
in the face

of this I want
to slide into

this great
grim maw

with the grace
of the gator

as he eases
himself onto

the bank
in the sun

and creaks
and smiles

just like
someone

settling into
a leather sofa

The Creeps

today is just
like yesterday

except for
a swim

across
the lake

whose water
creeps

me out most
always has

since long ago
when I first

discerned
the rusty

devil's claws
in the shallows

under my
canoe

that seemed
to strain to leap

from the lake
bed up

to drag
me and my

tipsy craft
down in

their jagged
clutch

nevertheless
I jump

into the cold
black

water and tie
the swim

ring to my
ankle in case

of cramp
or worse what

could be worse
I'll tell you

it's when
you reach

the deep
interior

a quarter
mile

from either
solid shore

and that
dark beast

who's kept
to those

silent depths
forever

will look up
and notice

above him
in the blue

a feast
two naked legs

winking whitely
in the high

firmament
of his world

and who will
surely rise

to investigate
what might

be for him
a revelation

of flavor
and swirl

akin
to that

of an oyster
or maybe

a pearl
on toast

Wild Raspberry

on a muggy
summer day

in a very
buggy berry

patch
you find

a fine
plump

jewel
and reach

for it when
over there!

a huge
and dazzling

juicier morsel
bigger than

your thumb
hanging by

a spider's
thread!

but as
you tug

on the now
humble nub

the sublimer
number falls

and is lost
forever

in that
murky

hole in
the dark

precarious
mess of

wet slash
and roots

beneath your
sorry feet

O

mountainous
appetite!

how flat
we'd find

the view
without you!

Littoral

A dragonfly
alights

beside me
on the dock

and cocks
his head

the better
to observe

the inert
and reddening

barge of flesh
looming large

above him
on this flawless

bright and windy
afternoon he's

not the flashy
type dull brown

with compound
ashy eyes

a bit rotunder
than the sky

blue dancer
with the black

and lacy wings
whose great

and fancy
beauty pings

the atmosphere
with instant

sapphire pleasure
when it deigns

to appear
and which

always brings
more than a whiff

of high art
to the party

I wonder
what he makes

of me this finely
bulging

little ounce
of God's intelligence

he might recall
Chagall's

Le Poète allongé
and rightly suspect

I'd imbibed a wee
bit too much wine

last night
or maybe

he admires
my complicated

hues the
perforated

subtle
light-thrown

shadows
the staccato

under the radar
the tonal score

of a lucky
poet who

on good days
understands

the soul as form
of forms who also

lives in fear
of the possibility

that the gods
might have

no need
for her at all

or maybe he's
just resting

in the sun
his manifold

eyes transmitting
sixty million

times this vision
to his tiny

conscious mind:
light

on the horizon
that ever-porous

littoral where
the bright

bleeds through
the borders

of the darkening
shore

Hybrid

all the new
thinking is

about energy
says my

new lover
as I wonder

about
the crowd

that hovers
in the green

inbetweenness
in my head

the energetic
crew who

speak unspoken to
who volunteer

non sequiturs
when I'm mining

for the deeper thing
the regal thing

they substitute
gumshoe hoedown

or *a fine toothcomb*
or if I ponder

a smart sonnet
on *The Institute*

of Forgetting
they'll offer

moth-eaten
feather-bedded

meat-balled
things then steer

me into Beer
Harbor and say

y'on y'one
and leave

me sprawled
unhouseled

in hybrid doubt
about the rough

and tumble of
this banquet hall

when all
I really itch

to do is
engrave

on a golden bowl
a soliloquy

on the physics
of the soul

that hilarious
white wave

on the tufted
dark of the sea

Peony

Plump mother-lode
of pleasure

tight buds all
awash in ants

pink skirts ragged
at the edges

old-fashioned
bowl

of fragrance
palace of ants

and feathers
I watch

the rain come
and the shining

heads bow
under heavy

jewels
Petals fall

in clumps
and scatter

soft and slow
on the pock-

marked soil
I cup a blossom

in my hands
lower my head and

inhale the scent
of *mother mother mother*

Stuck

the great blue
heron balances

on water
weeds

and pulls
at a long

dead stick
I've seen

him fly
these relics

into the high
dead tree

to build
his rigid nest

but this one
is truly stuck

no

he's pulling
at the body

of a cornsnake
whose tail

is knotted
firmly around

the stick his
head and half

his body
already

far down
the gullet

the heron can't
unknot the tail

so he
regurgitates

the top half
to work

a better angle
and now

the snake
dangles

limply as
the great bird

gnaws the gold-
red knot

with his hard
yellow beak

and swallows
again

an hour passes
the bird works

the cornsnake
clings the sun

shines
the wind

blows kites
and egrets

hawks and
swallows

soar in
the brilliant

light
of this

design
in which

every
bird

and every
beast

is obliged
to feast

on the living
to live

Run-on   *I.M.* Hugh Ogden

caveat emptor:

we'll be running
on together

for a while
and I'll

be carving up
the spiritual

possibilities in
the background

and we might
find from time

to time a reprise
of that old sublime

and unhappy opera
The Roaring

Desire for More
which is after all

the dire
wilderness

we all tend
to navigate

with tender
regard for

our poor
poor hands

so here's the plan
I'll serve as

the bravura conduit
to intuitionland

and you provide
the filthy lucre

and we'll orchestrate
a balanced dance

accompanied perhaps
by some nuanced

romantic fumbling
and maybe even

some Christian
death-threats

from the right
side of the brain

which is the nurse
douloureux

of macaronic
verse

o caro babbino now
don't you feel

better? not really
that nurse is standing

on her histrionic
feet and yelling that

a wolfowitz in shit's
clothing is marauding

in our fold a vast
and uncurtailed

misprision of vision
o la! le pauvre

he and his pals
ace the tests

of violence and shame
every time they take

them then they
stash the crude

oil under the bed
what a tired old

cliché they
should be taking

care of the waifs
and the orphans

instead they
congregate

at the mouth
of the bible factory

outlet I *ask* you
what is this great

and golden whirl
a-coming to? or

what is the chief
effect of this pageant

as Mr. Stevens very late
of Hartford asks

as did my great
friend Hugh

more newly late
of Hartford gone

on New Year's Eve
he strapped on

skis and glided
over the thinnest

merest whisper
of new ice

which failed him
then immobilizing

cold gathered
him slow

in its heavy
arms and now

on this the brighter
side of the divide

we're poorer by
one vivid loving

slight and wiry
barefoot man

bandannaed
wild-haired fond

of smoke and poems
and I wonder how

the lanyard
of history

will tether this
single glazing loss

to the catalogue
of misery

it so surely
is compiling

in its always
forthcoming

great long
poem

My Istanbul

my great blue
metropolis

of shadow and
of molten

dream my city
whose fabric

is constructed
of curious timbres

manhole covers
and nimble

historical seams
my city where grit

and beauty flash
in the windows

in transcendent
flares that

february forth
their slow revelations

as great green
accelerating mystery

muscles up
from the depths

of the hurrying
Bosphorus currents

my schizophrenic
city passionate

in it melancholy
and its keen

acquisitive ache
it glowers brightly

in its layers
of wool and gray

stone and linens
a splendid symphony

in minor key
home to riven

souls and ragged
beggars home

to the many
instruments

of poetry home
to polyspeak

whose pyrotechnic
frigidities dazzle

the spirit it's
out of control

it's out of this
world and

absolutely
fine

Geep

The music
of the sleepy

day was
ravagingly

dull until
Michael reeled

up a *geep*
from the depths

of his considerable
intelligence

a *geep!*
a wonky blend

of goat and sheep
a medical medley

genetic fugue
they call *chimera*

another wholly
enthralling sound

we found
when googling *geep*

whose enharmonic
bleating in the end

rings oh so
sad the photo

on the screen
reveals a downcast

baby creature
neither here

nor there
two bold

and mordant
sets of chromosomes

whistling fortissimo
through its patch-work

hide a botched-up
map of silken hair

and wooly yellow
fur its forlorn

droopy ears
a study

in radical
embarrassment

I feel profoundly
sorry for this

border folly
this lonely little

instrument
of the ever-

expanding notion
of what's possible

but then I see
we're kin

the little *geep* and me
we're marginal

ephemera
intoning low

invisible messages
at the edges

of the known
to who knows

whom
the difference

between us
a matter of degree

the poet of course
a hybrid creature

of transport and remorse
an over-reacher

in semaphore
who knows that sound's

the gold in the ore
whose pleasure-ground

is linguistic welter
that rides like ice

on its own melting
to paradise

or to a stranger land
we don't yet understand

from *Bird Book* (2017)

first green flare

makes
the air

quiver
and dart

the throat
ache

to call
makes

the heart
cheer

the ear
keen

to the sheer
glorious

windfall
of oriole

veery
vireo

A Bird

is a word
abroad

in air
on a stem

with roots
a gem

in scarlet
lemon

brown
the fruit

of import
from above

a weather
report

in short
a swift noun

a small
requiem

for all
that passes—

love
wind

grasses

Burrowing Owl

Very odd,
this little cloud

in trousers
in the sandy

fortress
favored by

prairie dog
and gopher

tortoise.
On the mound

at the mouth-hole,
he scouts around

with sibylline
yellow eyes

and then, owl-
wise, decides

to clean house.
He dives down

and soon
great clouds

of smudge come
flying out,

his home now
clean as a bone.

A diurnal owl,
he's upside-down

and inside-out,
at ease

not in trees,
but underground,

where his mate
broods

on her eight
fragile moons

in an immaculate
burrow whose

contours are lined
with cow manure.

Birds

are made
mostly of air.

They bear
scant weight

and many bright
colors. Eschewing

the freight
of matrimony,

they rarely mate
for life.

They lay
their speckled

eggs on stony
cliffs, on sea-wrack

or bare sand,
and in the grass.

Glass, alas,
often breaks

their necks
as they migrate

at night,
or in the bright

betrayals
of sunlight.

Indigo Bunting

blue as paint
blue as flame

blue as blue dawn
blue as the burn

after lightning
blue on fire

blue and a black beak
blue on electric wire

blue as the sky
just after dark

blue on the back
of the eye

blue as sleep
blue as a skyblue

dancer no bluer
blue as a sunning shark

blue as Nolde's
watercolor

blue shot
blue bead

bluer than the deep
indigo sea

blue as speed
blue fizz

blue black blue
dart and sizzle

Marsh Poodle

Absurd,
this watermark

shore-bird
who rackets

about, barking
like a yappy

poodle.
The black-

necked stilt
picks at

its food
with a needle-

thin bill
in knee-

deep water
as it hunts

by sight
for brine flies

and snails.
Long and

slender legs,
divinely

pink, trail
way behind

in flight.
You'd think

the stilt
was built

for speed,
but no,

it's pedigreed
in wading.

It saunters, or,
funnily, runs,

sprinkling
its way through

the shallows,
knees and ankles

bent backward
in liquid angles.

The truth is,
in its striking

and elegant
black-and-

white suit,
it's oddly

godly, and
beautiful

to the core,
as it bruits

about, spangling
the shore

Cardinal

His head
isn't red,

it's black
as a scalded

sinner.
He's bald

and pitiful,
but brave,

as he picks
at his seeds

from the eminence
of the feeder,

a shaved
and wincing

avian prince
at his dinner.

What turns
a song-bird

vulturine?
cap too tight?

territorial fight?
a terrible flaw

in the grand design?
A cuckoo pope?

Nope.
Feather mites.

Killdeer Bathing

Distinctive
black collar

invisible,
he wriggles,

frisky,
in the drink.

He prinks
and sprinkles

dizzy
droplets

everywhere
in the morning

air. Restored,
he resumes

his chores—
the brisk

and worried
survey

of the shore,
the skitter,

feint,
and twist

of the natural
catastrophist.

Whimbrel

Kin to
the limpkin,

she whimpers
when primping,

wears rimless
eyeglasses

for skimming
her primer

on swimming.
She splashes

through grasses
amassing

her rations
of shrimp,

and stands,
a fat ampersand,

on the sandpaper
strand

making eyes
at a snipe,

fanning
the passions

of the sandpiper
nation.

Turkey Vultures

lack a syrinx,
so cannot sing.

They really stink.
Their red heads

are featherless
for cleanliness.

They have three sets
of eyelashes.

They wash
their pinkish

legs in rivulets
of urine,

which stain
them white

and cool
them down.

They rule
many skies.

Generic name:
Cathartes.

Purifier.
When they fly,

they soar
for hours,

riding high
thermals,

gliding
on bountiful

rivers of air.
Tippy in flight,

they balance
and right,

hover and crown.
Pacific

creatures,
catholic

in their taste
for carrion,

they do not fight
or kill their prey.

Their feet
are clawed,

but weak,
as are their beaks.

They are benign
and much maligned.

Glory Train

Cleaning
house,

I find, in
a dried-out

flower
of brown

froth,
the tiny

skeleton
of a bat.

I set it on
a white plate

and tweeze
debris

from its frame.
The hand-

wing bones
are thin

as veins—
a miracle

of design,
fine almost

to vanishing,
the ephemeral

on which
so much

depends.
The pelvis

is small
as a pushpin,

frailer than
eggshell;

the fragile
vestibule

of the ribs
is clean and

unbroken.
It harbors

eight
desiccated

larvae that had,
rather late,

hopped
aboard

this darkly
upholstered

glory train.
The miniscule

figure hints
at the beautiful

old rhyme
of moon

and ruin,
the darkness

in which
constellated

hungers twitch
and fly,

feed on each
other and die.

Birding at the Hamilton County
Phosphate Mines

The plunder
of the vast

pine woods
has sundered

earth's live
crust

from rock.
The earth

has been stripped
and flayed,

and great
white mounds

of chalky
phosphogypsum

loom, giant,
poisonous

breasts,
over milky

waste-clay
ponds. Here

thousands
and thousands

of birds
perch and swim,

dabble, soar,
and dive.

Hawk, duck,
stork, sora,

ahninga,
sparrow,

wren—
all thrive

in this
humming

mess.
Sorrow

yields
to dubious

wonder
at the fecund,

blowzy
zen.

Bird Words

tanager
gnat-catcher

caspian tern
goat-sucker

chimney swift
canvasback

erne
bristle-thighed

curlew and
mandarin duck

fly like
the heartstrings

the stricken
and plucked

bunting
and oriole

veery
and lark

sing for
the deepest down

gold in the dark
godwit

and goldfinch
and stilt

on the fly
give me a gannet

to gladden
the eye

sora and
phalarope

phoebe
and kite

dicksissel
sapsucker

flicking
the night

magnificent
frigatebird

pinions
unfurled

the light
and the feathered

heart verbs
of the world

Loon

Designed
in cold

beautiful lines.
Brilliantined

black head,
fire-red eyes

that defy
the darkness

of the water
in which it thrives.

In pure lines
it dives

for lively
prey, lightning

in black,
as it sweeps

its waterways
with piercing eyes.

At home in deep
cold water,

at home in the dome
of the sky,

at home in flight
as it roams

from summer
to winter,

its unearthly cries
haunt our sleep.

They bring splinters
of wildness

to our nights
as we navigate

through dreams
and the streaming

wakes of the trails
we earthlings make.

Blue

The great blue
song of the earth
is sung in all
the best venues—
treetop, marsh,
desert, shore—
and on this spring
day in the wetlands
where, under
a late sun,
we stand alone
and in love
with each other
and the passing day
we watch a cormorant
whose eye is ringed
in blue diamonds,
a shimmering lure,
and we love this blue
and this dark bird
and this deepening sky
that pinks and hums
in the west, and then

the bird opens his beak
and flutters his throat
and the late
afternoon light
illuminates
the inside tissue
of his mouth

which is as blue
as his ocular jewelry,
as blue as the bluest
ocean, as blue
as the sky in all
its depth, as blue
as the back of the small
and determined beetle
who struggles to roll
his enormous dung ball
in his own breeding bid
to enchant another
small blue miracle

Osprey and Needlefish

The raptor
plunges

and clasps
in yellow talons

a thrashing
slender ribbon

of scale
and bone,

almost
too large

for its grasp.
They lisp

through
sunglare—

now up,
now down—

the fish
drowning

in air,
gasping

brute flesh,
until

the osprey
firms

control,
rights course,

the struggling
needlefish

a shuddering
keel

and they gain
altitude

and wheel
into the woods

where a brood
of wide-

mouthed heads
awaits

its lively
silver food

Birding at the Dairy

We're searching
for the single

yellow-headed
blackbird

we've heard
commingles

with thousands
of starlings

and brown-headed
cowbirds,

when the many-
headed body

arises
and undulates,

a sudden congress
of wings

in a maneuvering
wave that veers

and wheels, a fleet
and schooling swarm

in synchronous alarm,
a bloom radiating

in ribbons, in sheets,
in waterfall,

a murmuration
of birds

that turns
liquid in air,

that whooshes
like waves

on the shore,
or the breath

of a great
seething prayer.

thirty white

pelicans kettle
up in the sky

lazing in helical
praise of high

thermals which
hold them circling

pinned
to the pellicle

of blue film
between skin

and all things
angelical

The Hard Saving

for the Conservation Stewards of the
Alachua Conservation Trust

The sun hums low on a steaming river.
A late light whispers through littering oaks.
The long hours speak in the tongues of birds,
in the slip of leaves to the listening ground.

This earth-sprung language, bright and resonant,
rattles from the throats of the leaving cranes;
it springs from abundant shining waters
as they lunge for distant mangrove shores;

it pours in the dialect of thundering rain
which adds to the fund of the mother tongue,
the source that lies low, transparent and full,
the life-stream, the fundament, the great clear heart.

In full fine words the earth is speaking
to those who listen and care to respond.
But the subtle words are harder to hear
and harder to find and smaller. It's late.

Those who listen hear time stutter short,
hear squeals of profit shatter the peace.
The living words say *It's time, it's time,*
put by the fragile growing treasure.

This saving is hard. There's hard labor in thrift.
But those who listen have been resourceful.
Some savings have accumulated and we are richer
for tenacious accounting of the living green.

We still have incomparable deep-voiced springs,
big river-making and brilliant sources,
tall grasses still whisper their shining songs,
dark nights are still lit by singing creatures.

Yet we must save more of our oldest reserve,
we must learn to balance trust and power;
we must sing the economy of saving grace,
we must continue that song and not stop saving.

Notes

Figure and Ground: Cryptic Camouflage and Visual Rhyme. The first stanza is reprinted with permission from *The Stokes Field Guide to the Birds of North America,* by Donald and Lillian Stokes. New York: Little, Brown, and Company, 2010.

Swan Lake. Inspired by a chapter in Emily Post's 1941 edition of *Etiquette* entitled "Calling on a Lady Who Has No Maid."

Apostrophe to, and Roses for, Beatrice. All of the capitalized words in the poem are trademarked rose names.

The Combine. After Elizabeth Bishop's "The Moose."

Bricolage. Cf Lesley Blanch's *The Wilder Shores of Love*.

Dancing at the *Binbir Gece*. "Binbir Gece" means "the thousand and one nights."

Geep. The final sonnet is indebted to Robert Frost's essay, "The Figure a Poem Makes."

Acknowledgments

I am grateful to the editors of the following journals, where some of these new poems have been previously published:

American Journal of Poetry: "The Wood Stork" (originally published as "The Undertaker")
The Arkansas International: "Fata Morgana"
Birmingham Poetry Review: "Fabric"
Blackbird: "Fear" (originally published as "Bees, Return")
Plume: "Seeing the Ophthalmologist," "Skin," "Eye"

And immense gratitude to all who have helped me make my poems over the years and who have inspired me to continue the study and consideration and praise that comprise, for me, the writing of poetry. To my Poultry Group— Lola Haskins, Joe Haldeman, Brandy Kershner; to my helpful and constant friends—Geoff Brock, Randall Mann, Michael Loughran, Lisa Zeidner; and to Wyatt Prunty and the incomparable Sewanee Summer Writers' Conference and all its remarkable staff, faculty, and students, I owe more than I can possibly say. Thank you.

About the Author: Sidney Wade's seventh collection of poems, *Bird Book*, was published by Atelier26 Books in September 2017. She is professor emerita of creative writing at the University of Florida, where she taught MFA@FLA program workshops in poetry and translation for 23 years. A past president of the Association of Writers and Writing Programs, she is also the former secretary/treasurer of the American Literary Translators Association. Her translation with Efe Murad of *Silent Stones: Selected Poems of Melih Cevdet Anday* won the Meral Divitçi Prize for Turkish Poetry in Translation and was published by Talisman House in April 2017. She served as poetry editor for the literary journal *Subtropics* for many years, and her poems and translations have appeared in a wide variety of journals, including *Poetry, The New Yorker, Grand Street,* and *The Paris Review,* as well as many other literary publications.

Poetry Titles in the Series

John Hollander, *Blue Wine and Other Poems*

Robert Pack, *Waking to My Name: New and Selected Poems*

Philip Dacey, *The Boy under the Bed*

Wyatt Prunty, *The Times Between*

Barry Spacks, *Spacks Street, New and Selected Poems*

Gibbons Ruark, *Keeping Company*

David St. John, *Hush*

Wyatt Prunty, *What Women Know, What Men Believe*

Adrien Stoutenberg, *Land of Superior Mirages: New and Selected Poems*

John Hollander, *In Time and Place*

Charles Martin, *Steal the Bacon*

John Bricuth, *The Heisenberg Variations*

Tom Disch, *Yes, Let's: New and Selected Poems*

Wyatt Prunty, *Balance as Belief*

Tom Disch, *Dark Verses and Light*

Thomas Carper, *Fiddle Lane*

Emily Grosholz, *Eden*

X. J. Kennedy, *Dark Horses: New Poems*

Wyatt Prunty, *The Run of the House*

Robert Phillips, *Breakdown Lane*

Vicki Hearne, *The Parts of Light*

Timothy Steele, *The Color Wheel*

Josephine Jacobsen, *In the Crevice of Time: New and Collected Poems*

Thomas Carper, *From Nature*

John Burt, *Work without Hope: Poetry by John Burt*

Charles Martin, *What the Darkness Proposes: Poems*

Wyatt Prunty, *Since the Noon Mail Stopped*

William Jay Smith, *The World below the Window: Poems 1937–1997*

Wyatt Prunty, *Unarmed and Dangerous: New and Selected Poems*

Robert Phillips, *Spinach Days*

X. J. Kennedy, *The Lords of Misrule: Poems 1992–2001*

John T. Irwin, ed., *Words Brushed by Music: Twenty-Five Years of the Johns Hopkins Poetry Series*

John Bricuth, *As Long As It's Big: A Narrative Poem*

Robert Phillips, *Circumstances Beyond Our Control: Poems*

Daniel Anderson, *Drunk in Sunlight*

X. J. Kennedy, *In a Prominent Bar in Secaucus: New and Selected Poems, 1955–2007*

William Jay Smith, *Words by the Water*

Wyatt Prunty, *The Lover's Guide to Trapping*

Charles Martin, *Signs & Wonders*

Peter Filkins, *The View We're Granted*

Brian Swann, *In Late Light*

Daniel Anderson, *The Night Guard at the Wilberforce Hotel*

Wyatt Prunty, *Couldn't Prove, Had to Promise*

John Bricuth, *Pure Products of America, Inc.*

X. J. Kennedy, *That Swing: Poems 2008–2016*

Charles Martin, *Future Perfect*

Hastings Hensel, *Ballyhoo*

Sidney Wade, *Deep Gossip: New and Selected Poems*

CPSIA information can be obtained
at www.ICGtesting.com
Printed in the USA
BVHW032114070420
577150BV00001B/106